# CHAPTER 1:

The Fascination of Coffee Shop Ventures

Coffee shops—spaces brimming with an enticing mixture of aromatic drinks, mouth-watering edibles, and a friendly environment. In this initial exploration, we will delve into the intrigue of the coffee shop industry and why it enthralls budding entrepreneurs.

Global Rise of the Coffee Connoisseur: In recent times, the appreciation for coffee has transitioned from being a simple daily routine to a worldwide craze. Coffee shops are no longer just pit-stops for a caffeine fix, but rather central hubs for social interaction, productivity, and leisure. The captivating smell of freshly brewed coffee, the inviting atmosphere, and the opportunity to enjoy a peaceful respite in the middle of a busy day have propelled the popularity of coffee culture.

Canvas for Innovation and Originality: Coffee shops often serve as breeding grounds for creativity. Whether it's the detailed patterns on a frothy latte or the distinctive interiors that mirror the shop's identity, these spaces offer a platform for showcasing artistic talent. The prospect of intertwining a love for coffee with a knack for creativity is an enticing proposition for many coffee shop proprietors.

Masters of Memorable Interactions: Coffee shops are more than just dispensers of drinks; they're curators of unique experiences. The joy of designing memorable interactions—from the first exhilarating sip of a signature brew to a spirited conversation with a barista—adds a fulfilling dimension to coffee shop entrepreneurship. Creating a place where customers feel comfortable and can relish the moment brings immense satisfaction to coffee shop owners.

Centers for Community Engagement: One of the most rewarding aspects of running a coffee shop is the potential to nurture community relationships. Coffee shops often evolve into communal hubs where locals, friends, and coworkers convene to share experiences and establish bonds. The sense of unity that a coffee shop can foster is genuinely special. The opportunity to shape a space that becomes an indispensable part of people's daily routines is a potent motivator for coffee shop owners.

Nurturing a Coffee Obsession: For many coffee shop owners, their passion for coffee is the primary catalyst for their entry into this industry. Owning a coffee shop provides a platform to share this passion, enlighten customers about the diverse world of coffee—from its varied types to its complex tasting notes. The continual journey of exploring new coffee blends and perfecting brewing techniques adds a constant source of intrigue and inspiration.

The fascination of coffee shop ventures is rooted in the sensory pleasures of coffee, the fusion of creative expression, the gratification of crafting memorable interactions, the sense of unity, and the constant exploration of the coffee universe. As you embark on your coffee shop entrepreneurship journey, keep in mind the intrinsic allure that captivates customers, guiding you to construct a place that leaves an indelible mark on their memories.

# CHAPTER 2:

## Understanding the Coffeehouse Business Landscape

### The Advantages and Risks

Coffeehouses, with their enchanting charm, often appear as the perfect entrepreneurial dream. Yet, the route to this dream is sprinkled with both opportunities and potential challenges. This chapter delves into the varying aspects of running a coffeehouse, giving you an insight into the vibrant yet demanding landscape of this venture.

Positive Aspects of the Coffeehouse Venture: A Conduit for Originality: A coffeehouse is a stage where you can choreograph your creativity. The interior, menu, and overall ambiance can be curated to reflect your signature style and ethos.

Cultivating Social Bonds: Coffeehouses are known for being the heart of a community. As an owner, you get to host and foster relationships within the neighborhood, creating a warm and familiar meeting point for patrons.

Coffee Connoisseurship: If coffee runs in your veins, a coffeehouse lets you dive deeper into its world. It's an opportunity to discover and introduce diverse blends and brewing techniques, and share your passion with your clientele.

Entrepreneurial Autonomy: As a coffeehouse owner, you dictate your work schedule and business strategies, giving you a sense of freedom and control.

Potential for Profit: With careful management, a coffeehouse can turn into a profitable venture, bringing financial success alongside the joy of running a business.

Challenging Aspects of the Coffeehouse Venture: Market Competition: The coffeehouse industry teems with competitors, both new and established. Creating a niche and attracting a steady flow of customers requires out-of-the-box marketing and exceptional services.

Initial Investment: Opening a coffeehouse necessitates a significant upfront investment. From leasing a prime location to hiring and training staff, managing the finances can be a daunting task for newcomers.

Intensive Time Commitment: Running a coffeehouse often calls for long hours, especially during peak times. The constant need to cater to early morning rush and late-night coffee lovers can pose challenges to your work-life balance.

Seasonal Inconsistencies: Depending on location and customer habits, coffeehouses may see fluctuations in foot traffic and earnings. These ups and downs require a level of resilience and strategic planning to keep the business afloat.

Workforce Management: Maintaining a competent and motivated staff aligned with your coffeehouse's ethos is a constant endeavor. Frequent changes in staff and training needs can affect the overall customer experience and require continuous attention.

As enticing as starting a coffeehouse can be, it's a journey marked with unique opportunities and challenges. Understanding these aspects, coupled with a robust business plan and a thorough understanding of your market, can set you on a path to creating a successful and fulfilling coffeehouse venture.

# CHAPTER 4:

## Unraveling the Industry Landscape: A Deep Dive into Coffee Shop Market Research and Viability Analysis

A coffee shop's success hinges on thorough market research, providing insights into the industry, performance metrics, and trending concepts. It also aids in fine-tuning business facets to captivate the right clientele.

Let's walk through the essential phases of comprehensive market research for your coffee shop venture.

Purposes of Coffee Shop Market Research

Market research encompasses several fundamental goals:

Market Evaluation: The market saturation level and demand for coffee shops should be assessed. Ponder over questions like:

- Is the local demand for coffee exceeding the supply?
- Are there untapped customer segments?
- Are there areas that are deprived of a coffee shop like the one you envision?
- Is your chosen location conducive to a new coffee shop?

Target Audience Identification: The gathered data aids in pinpointing a concept that resonates with your target customers. Proximity to educational institutions or business districts could influence your customer base, necessitating adaptations to their tastes, routines, and requirements.

Sales Potential Assessment: Gather data to gauge the prospective sales of your coffee shop.

Essential Areas for Coffee Shop Market Research

Kickstart your market research by concentrating on three key areas:

Audience and Product Alignment: Ascertain the best-suited products and services for your target audience.

Competitive Advantage: Strategize on capturing market share from rivals and distinguishing your coffee shop from existing local eateries.

Customer Attraction and Loyalty: Formulate strategies for drawing and retaining customers and develop a dynamic marketing strategy that continually keeps your coffee shop on the customer's mind.

Market Trends to Monitor

Effective market research demands a meticulous analysis of market trends, customer expectations, and a thorough understanding of applicable regulations. Here are a few aspects to consider during your coffee shop market research:

Industry Dynamics: Gauge if the coffee shop market is expanding or shrinking and analyze turnover trends.

Business Hurdles: Identify common challenges faced by coffee shop operators, such as supply chain issues or the recruitment and retention of skilled staff.

Customer Preferences: Understand the current consumption patterns of coffee shop patrons, their demographics, average expenditure per customer, and preferred products. Connect with local coffee shop owners and customers for insights into their preferences and motivations.

Regulatory Compliance: Familiarize yourself with the laws governing coffee shop operations during your market research. Ensure compliance to establish and run your coffee shop successfully.

Analyzing Local Demand for Coffee Shops

With a solid grasp of the coffee shop sector, focus on the local market attributes, where you plan to set up your shop. Start by estimating the local market size, the population's demographic profile, and how much of it is your target audience. Consider factors like age, gender, employment status, and disposable income.

Take into account how often people frequent the area where you plan to operate your coffee shop. Identify specific locations within the local market with the potential to draw maximum footfall. These could be bustling shopping streets, office vicinities, or picturesque seaside locations.

Finally, gauge local customer preferences. Is there a unique beverage or snack demand currently unfulfilled?

Assessing the Competition

A comprehensive analysis of local competition is integral to market research. Compile a list of all eateries in the vicinity and scrutinize their concepts, product offerings, pricing strategy, and target clientele. Understand their space, seating capacity, employee count, and turnover.

Take note of the reputation of your competitors as well. Interact with local business owners and residents to gather opinions on their product quality and customer service. Allocate time to read online reviews and ratings.

Studying Customer Attraction Strategies

Evaluate your competitors' key strategies for drawing and retaining customers. Analyze their marketing practices to develop a unique marketing strategy tailored to your specific target audience.

Feasibility Analysis for Your Coffee Shop

Financial Projections: Develop detailed financial forecasts, including initial costs, ongoing expenses, revenue predictions, and potential profitability. Account for rent, utilities, payroll, ingredient costs, marketing expenses, and projected sales volume.

Break-Even Analysis: Carry out a break-even analysis to ascertain the point at which your total revenue will cover all costs.

Risk Evaluation: Identify potential risks that might impact your business, such as market saturation, evolving consumer tastes, economic downturns, or regulatory shifts. Formulate contingency plans to manage these risks.

Operational Factors: Assess the operational demands of running a coffee shop, including staffing requirements, supply chain management, equipment maintenance, and customer service.

Customer Feedback: Conduct surveys and focus groups to collect direct feedback from your target market on coffee shop preferences, menu offerings, pricing, ambiance, and customer service.

Test Your Concept: Consider a soft launch or pop-up events to evaluate customer response to your coffee shop concept.

Online Engagement: Monitor online platforms and social media to understand customer sentiment, reviews, and discussions related to coffee shops in your target market.

By understanding your target market, evaluating the competition, assessing location viability, preparing financial forecasts, and gathering customer feedback, you can craft a resilient business strategy. This thorough analysis can increase the likelihood of your coffee shop resonating with customers, meeting their needs, and thriving in a competitive marketplace.

# CHAPTER 5:

## Crafting an Astute Strategy for Your Cafe Venture

Venturing into the cafe business can be a thrilling journey filled with rewards, but it mandates diligent planning and structuring. A meticulous business strategy serves as the North Star, guiding your cafe towards future prosperity. In this chapter, we'll walk you through the stages of constructing an all-encompassing business strategy for your cafe, addressing fundamental elements that lay the groundwork for your enterprise.

Strategic Blueprint: Think of the strategic blueprint as the trailer to your business's movie. It should be brief yet compelling, providing a snapshot of your business plan. Embed a succinct depiction of your cafe's concept, potential market, competitive edge, and financial forecasts. The aim is to pique curiosity and invite further exploration into your plan.

Business Characterization and Conceptualization: Give a vivid portrayal of your cafe, encompassing its branding, location, legal form, and core purpose. Elucidate on your cafe's conceptualization, focusing on the kind of culinary experience or unique beverages you'll provide, the ambiance, and the overall customer journey you wish to design.

Market Evaluation: Execute an exhaustive market study to comprehend your prospective market, competition, and industry shifts. Pinpoint your ideal customer group, their demography, inclinations, and spending patterns. Evaluate the competition in the spectrum, from cafes to restaurants and bakeries, dissecting their strong and weak points. Use this data to spot voids and chances in the market that your cafe can exploit.

Food and Beverage Portfolio: Elucidate your food and beverage portfolio in depth. Incorporate a broad spectrum of choices, taking into account dietary needs, prevailing food trends, and customer likings. Discuss any peculiar or signature items that make your cafe distinct. Consider aspects like sourcing top-notch ingredients, pricing tactics, and potential suppliers.

Promotion and Sales Tactics: Enumerate your approach to promotion and sales that aims to lure and hold onto customers. Define your market segments and develop tactics to effectively communicate with them. Sketch your branding strategy, including logo creation, website design, social media engagement, and promotional campaigns. Explore local alliances, community involvement, and customer loyalty programs.

Operational Blueprint: Describe the routine operations of your cafe, ranging from working hours, staffing needs, to the workflow sequence. Outline the roles and responsibilities of key personnel, including the management team, culinary experts, baristas, and service staff. Incorporate data about required licenses and permits, health and safety standards, and any distinctive operational elements specific to your cafe.

Financial Estimation: Formulate a comprehensive financial strategy that includes initial investment, income projections, and expense forecasts. Identify your funding sources, whether self-funding, loans, or investors, and set a realistic budget. Take into account aspects like rent, equipment, inventory, employee salaries, promotional expenses, and recurring operational costs. Use financial estimations to gauge profitability, cash management, and return on investment.

SWOT Evaluation: Execute a SWOT (Strengths, Weaknesses, Opportunities, Threats) evaluation to appraise internal and external factors that might influence your cafe. Recognize unique strengths and competitive advantages of your cafe, such as a prime spot or an exclusive menu. Address shortcomings, like limited parking or fierce competition, and formulate strategies to overcome them. Identify potential growth areas, such as broadening catering services or collaborations with local enterprises. Lastly, recognize possible threats, such as economic fluctuations or shifting consumer trends, and devise contingency plans.

Risk Evaluation and Management: Analyze potential risks and challenges that your cafe might encounter and devise strategies to manage them. Reflect on aspects like market oversaturation, food safety norms, staffing issues, or unforeseen circumstances like natural calamities. Develop backup plans to guarantee the sustainability and resilience of your cafe venture.

Drafting a comprehensive business strategy is a crucial stride in launching a successful cafe. It offers clarity, direction, and a solid basis for your enterprise. By considering each component outlined in this chapter, you'll be well-equipped to maneuver the challenges and capitalize on the opportunities on the horizon. Ensure to routinely reassess and refresh your business strategy as your cafe evolves, allowing it to remain a dynamic and potent instrument for your business's expansion.

# CHAPTER 6:

Embarking on the Café Adventure: Translating Data into Decisions

In the Café Universe, your vision will pave the path to your destination. What will your café represent? Will it be a cozy community center, a trendy urban escape, or a lively social hub? Honing your vision will set the stage for your concept development journey.

After accumulating a plethora of insights through comprehensive café market scrutiny, the following course of action is to transform this knowledge into strategic maneuvers. The insights will act as your compass, guiding the decision-making and directing the trajectory of your café venture.

Formulating a Marketing Strategy The conception of your vision will be the stepping stone to devising tactics for customer acquisition and retention. Ascertain the most powerful methods to engage your target audience and weave them into a broad-based marketing game plan. This plan should mirror your business objectives and address your customer needs, encapsulating various channels such as social media, your website, local promotions, and potential partnerships with allied businesses.

Conceptualization and Market Viability Assessment Your market analysis might hint that the market might be saturated, or your initial business proposition does not resonate with customer demands. It's crucial to acknowledge these roadblocks and recalibrate your plan of action. Conversely, the right set of data might unlock a profitable business avenue for your café. In this case, the first stepping stone would be to sculpt a potent concept for your café. This concept should be designed to cater to a specific demographic, delivering a service that not only fulfills their needs but also sets you apart from the crowd.

Conducting a Quantitative Study to Validate Your Concept Before plunging into substantial financial commitments, it's advisable to conduct a quantitative study to examine your concept among potential customers. This study will not only help in presenting a realistic snapshot of your offerings to a large customer base, thereby authenticating your concept but also provide an opportunity to tweak the concept, if required.

Designing the Café Concept Once your vision is clarified, the next step is to develop a consistent brand identity that echoes this vision. This will involve crafting an engaging brand narrative, designing an appealing logo, choosing a suitable color palette, and selecting fonts that mirror your café's personality.

Establishing a Unique Selling Proposition (USP) After your identity is set, the next focus should be on determining what gives your café a competitive advantage. Could it be a unique coffee assortment, a pledge to sustainable practices, a preference for locally-sourced ingredients, or an unmatched ambiance? Your USP will act as a customer magnet.

Crafting the Ambiance and Interior Design The next step in your journey involves developing a suitable ambiance by selecting a theme that strikes a chord with your target demographic. Consider factors such as lighting, music, furniture, and decor. Once the ambiance is set, optimize your café's layout to ensure both comfort and efficiency. Consider the strategic arrangement of seating to encourage social interaction or provide quiet corners for those seeking solitude.

Curating the Menu Design a diverse beverage menu that appeals to various preferences. Include a range of coffee options, and consider adding alternative milk choices and unique flavor combinations. Complement this with a carefully curated food menu that aligns with your audience's preferences, dietary restrictions, and current culinary trends.

Engaging with the Community Hosting events and workshops, forming alliances with local businesses, and showcasing your commitment to social causes are other significant aspects that can amplify the overall experience and create a unique identity for your café.

To summarize, by defining your vision, crafting a unique ambiance, devising a delightful menu, and engaging with your community, you can create a café experience that is unique. The concept you create becomes the heartbeat of your business, drawing customers in and fostering a loyal community.

# CHAPTER 7:

Uncovering the Ideal Café Location: A Strategic Guide

Finding the perfect location for your café business is like piecing together a complex puzzle. The quest might be marked by stumbling blocks such as a scarcity of viable locations, prohibitive rental rates, or challenging lease terms. Despite these challenges, it's crucial to keep your vision intact and take into account more than just rental costs and spatial considerations. Here are the top five aspects to ponder while selecting a location for your café venture:

Understanding the Customer Demographics The worth of foot traffic dwindles if the bustling crowd does not align with your target audience. Knowledge of your target demographic is crucial and should significantly steer your location selection. Identify the destinations of your potential customers and understand the motivations behind their purchasing decisions. If your primary target audience is office-goers seeking a caffeine fix before work, a café in a family-oriented shopping center may not yield desired sales despite the high foot traffic. A location close to a business district or an office park could be more profitable.

Deciphering the Influence of Neighboring Businesses The success of your café can be both positively and negatively affected by surrounding businesses. Your competition isn't confined to just other coffee shops. Consider other fast-food joints, juice bars, or bagel places that could be alternatives to your café for a quick breakfast. Conversely, businesses in the vicinity can complement your café too. For instance, if your café offers a conducive environment for studying or working, proximity to a university or businesses can attract the student or working population.

Prioritizing Accessibility The convenience of your café's location plays a significant role in attracting first-time customers, even if the quality of your coffee entices them to return. Consider how your target audience might reach your café. If your potential customers predominantly use cars, adequate parking becomes crucial. Alternatively, if they're walking, the café's visibility from the street becomes important. If your location is not easily accessible, you run the risk of losing customers to competitors.

Assessing Building Infrastructure Your café will require a specific building infrastructure that may not be possible in all commercial spaces. Look for a cozy yet spacious location that can accommodate your customers comfortably without making the place seem overcrowded. Ensure the place has ample room to set up café equipment and allows your baristas to move freely. Also, it's essential to inquire about the permits for food or alcohol, as there could be restrictions depending on the location. It might be beneficial to seek advice from a legal or business expert in this regard.

Considering Lease Terms Affordability is a prime factor when selecting a location. Ask yourself: Can I afford the rent and can my customers afford my coffee prices, which will reflect high rental costs? Be mindful of your customers' sensitivity to prices. Moreover, evaluate if the chosen location requires any renovations and if small business loans could aid in covering these expenses. When considering loan offers, look into the total repayment amount, repayment ease, and the lender's reputation. In addition to the cost of the property, understanding the lease terms can influence your decision. You need to understand the lease duration, permissible rent hikes, insurance stipulations, security deposit conditions, and terms for maintenance and repairs. Consulting with a legal expert can ensure you fully comprehend and adhere to the lease terms.

In conclusion, selecting a location for your café is a balancing act, considering several factors such as your target demographics, nearby businesses, accessibility, building infrastructure, and lease terms. With a strategic approach, you can find the location that fits perfectly with your café vision.

# CHAPTER 8:

## Designing a Captivating Café Menu: An Art and Science

The café menu serves as the heart of your customer's experience, reflecting the essence of your establishment, setting the stage for what you offer, and instilling expectations. A finely curated menu offers more than just a listing of your culinary creations and their prices – it informs, guides, and entices customers, driving meaningful engagements and fostering customer loyalty. Let's delve into the essential elements of crafting a captivating café menu.

Determining Your Café's Identity Before you venture into developing your menu, it's important to have a clear understanding of your café's identity – the concept you wish to project, your target audience, and how you envision your customers' interaction with your offerings. For instance, a drive-thru coffee shack focusing on milk-based beverages will adopt a different menu strategy compared to a cosmopolitan café known for its single-origin coffees. Knowing your café's persona shapes your menu.

Deciphering Customer Preferences Carry out thorough market research to understand your target audience's preferences, dietary needs, and current culinary trends. Gaining insights into their taste buds, budget, and openness to try innovative flavors will shape your menu creation process.

Structuring Your Menu The layout of your menu should cater to your audience's preferences. You could categorize your offerings by type (like beverages, breakfast, lunch, desserts), flavor profiles (sweet, savory, spicy), or dietary requirements (vegetarian, gluten-free). Ensure that your menu's organization is logical and user-friendly.

Carving Out Your Unique Identity While drawing inspiration from successful café menus can be helpful, it's crucial to carve out your unique identity. Spend time testing and perfecting your recipes to create a menu that truly represents your café's spirit. Consider all elements, from the size of the servings to the source of your ingredients to the names of your beverages. By doing so, you can confidently engage with customers about your offerings and ensure their satisfaction.

Designing the Menu Layout Your menu's design and layout significantly contribute to the customer's overall experience. Aim for simplicity and clarity. Avoid overwhelming your customers with a chaotic array of choices. Opt for a clear layout that displays your offerings at one price and size, with additional options or extras listed separately. Organize your menu similar to a newspaper layout, with the top left being the prime spot for your popular drinks, and structure the rest of the menu accordingly.

Curating a Diverse Beverage Menu Offer an array of coffee options, from espresso-based drinks to single-origin brews, and showcase their unique attributes. Cater to non-coffee drinkers with a selection of traditional and specialty teas, and other alternative beverages like matcha lattes or herbal infusions. Introduce seasonal specials to keep your menu exciting and encourage repeat visits.

Crafting a Balanced Food Menu Balance your food menu with options for all, accommodating different tastes and dietary needs. Use fresh, high-quality ingredients, source locally when feasible, and highlight any specialty ingredients. Create signature dishes that stand out and become synonymous with your café.

Designing and Presenting the Menu Design your menu with an attractive layout that mirrors your café's branding. Incorporate high-resolution photographs of your offerings and use font styles, colors, and graphics that align with your café's aesthetics. Describe your menu items vividly to paint a picture of their flavors, ingredients, and preparation methods. Set your pricing strategically based on costs, market trends, and competition, and use pricing tiers or bundles to add value and promote upselling. Remember, your pricing should reflect the quality and experience you deliver.

In conclusion, creating a café menu is a harmonious blend of art and science, requiring strategic planning, creative design, and an understanding of your customer preferences. A well-crafted menu can leave a lasting impression, driving customer loyalty and ensuring your café's success.

# CHAPTER 9:

### The Fundamental Steps for a Successful Café Launch

Investing in a café business is an electrifying adventure. Whether you are a coffee enthusiast wishing to share your passion or an ambitious entrepreneur aiming to tap into the expanding specialty beverage industry, owning the right set of tools and supplies is a prerequisite. This comprehensive guide is designed to shed light on the essential equipment and ingredients necessary to set up a prosperous café business.

Prioritizing a Functional and Appealing Café Space Before we plunge into the specifics of equipment and supplies, curating a café ambiance that is both inviting and efficient is key. Here are some factors to take into consideration:

Choosing Furniture and Aesthetic Touches A comfortable and inviting atmosphere stems from choosing the right furniture and décor. Opt for resilient tables, chairs, and cozy seating arrangements. Embellish the ambiance with striking decorations that echo your brand's theme.

Spotting the Right Location and Designing an Efficient Layout The first critical move is securing an optimal location for your café. After that, devise a layout that maximizes seating capacity without compromising customer flow.

Equipping Your Café To ensure your café operates smoothly, an array of specialized tools is needed. Here are some core pieces of equipment:

Commercial-grade Espresso Machine The espresso machine is at the heart of any café. Invest in a top-notch espresso machine designed to meet your business's demands. Look for features such as programmable settings, multiple group heads, and integrated grinders for a quick and uniform brewing process.

Additional Brewing Appliances Depending on your menu, you might need additional brewing tools like drip coffee makers, pour-over devices, or French presses. Research different options and choose those that align with your brewing style.

Commercial Cooling Units Keeping perishable items like milk, cream, and food ingredients fresh is essential. Therefore, invest in commercial-grade refrigerators and freezers that provide ample storage and temperature control.

Blenders and Mixers If your café plans to offer smoothies or blended drinks, you will need high-quality blenders and mixers. Choose models with varied speed settings and robust blades for effective blending.

Coffee Grinder For fresh, well-extracted coffee, a burr grinder that provides consistent grind size is crucial. Make sure it has adjustable settings to accommodate different brewing techniques.

Cleaning Station A well-equipped dishwashing station is necessary to maintain hygiene. This station should include a commercial dishwasher, sinks, and storage racks. Always comply with local health and safety regulations.

Keeping Stock of Quality Supplies and Ingredients In addition to equipment, you will need to source high-quality supplies and ingredients:

Coffee Beans The coffee beans you select greatly influence the flavor of your drinks. Source from trustworthy suppliers, and experiment with different blends to cater to varied tastes.

Milk and Dairy Substitutes Fresh milk and dairy substitutes like almond milk, soy milk, or oat milk are important for creamy coffee drinks. Cater to different dietary needs by offering a variety of options.

Flavor Enhancers A range of syrups and flavorings can amplify the taste profiles of your drinks. Keep classic options like vanilla, caramel, and hazelnut on hand, but also introduce seasonal or specialty flavors for variety.

Takeaway Supplies and Dine-In Utensils Stock necessary takeaway items like cups, lids, stirrers, and napkins. Additionally, invest in high-quality serve ware like mugs, glasses, and plates for dine-in customers.

Cleaning and Upkeep Maintain a high level of cleanliness and sanitation with cleaning supplies such as sanitizers, detergents, brushes, and cloths. Regularly servicing your equipment ensures its longevity and optimal performance.

Having the right tools and supplies is a fundamental step towards a successful café business. Invest in superior equipment, source premium ingredients, and craft an inviting ambiance for a memorable customer experience. Whether you're launching your café or revamping an existing one, prioritize quality, consistency, and customer satisfaction to thrive in the competitive market.

# CHAPTER 10:

Legal Foundations for a Successful Café Business

Embarking on a café business journey is a thrilling endeavor. However, before you can welcome customers into your space, it's important to lay a legal foundation by acquiring the necessary permits and licenses. Failure to do so could have serious repercussions, including penalties, business closure, or harm to your reputation. This chapter is designed to guide you through the web of permits and licenses required for a café business.

Grasping the Terminology Licenses and permits are authorizations provided by government bodies that allow individuals or businesses to perform certain operations. In the café context, these authorizations ensure your business aligns with standards for health, safety, and operations.

Forming a Legal Business Entity One of the first steps in opening a café is formalizing your business entity. Here's what that process might look like:

Business Registration: Start by declaring your café as a legal entity. The process requires you to select a business structure (such as a sole proprietorship, partnership, or LLC) and register it with the necessary government bodies.

Business License: You will need to acquire a business license, granting you legal authority to operate in a specific area. The process for obtaining this license differs by location, so it's important to consult with your local government or licensing authority.

Sales Tax Permit: If you intend to sell taxable goods or services, you will need a sales tax permit, allowing you to collect and remit sales tax to the relevant authority.

Navigating Health and Safety Rules A clean and safe environment is of paramount importance in the foodservice industry. To demonstrate compliance with health and safety regulations, you'll need to secure the following permits:

Food Service Permit: Any café that prepares and serves food must secure a food service permit, proving you adhere to local health department hygiene and safety standards.

Health Inspection: Your café will also undergo regular health inspections. These inspections evaluate the cleanliness of your facility, appropriate food handling practices, and adherence to health codes.

Fire Safety Permit: A fire safety permit is necessary to ensure the safety of your customers and staff. The local fire department issues this permit after inspecting your café for fire safety, including the presence of necessary fire safety equipment.

Additional Licenses (If Applicable) If your café will serve alcohol or feature outdoor seating, you will need to acquire additional permits:

Liquor License: If you plan to serve alcohol, you will need a liquor license. The process for obtaining this license can include background checks, financial disclosures, and meeting age and zoning requirements.

Alcohol Server Certification: In some jurisdictions, those serving alcohol must have an alcohol server certification. This certification assures servers are familiar with responsible alcohol service guidelines, including recognizing signs of intoxication and preventing underage drinking.

Outdoor Seating Permits: If you plan to offer outdoor seating, make sure you're aware of any necessary permits and safety regulations in your area.

Other Permits to Consider Lastly, your café might require these additional permits:

Signage Permits: To display signage promoting your café, you might need a permit. Check with your local zoning or planning department to understand any restrictions on signage.

Music Licensing: If you intend to play music in your café, ensure you have the proper music licenses from organizations like performance rights organizations (PROs) and music licensing companies.

Navigating the process of acquiring the necessary licenses and permits for your café business can seem daunting, but with proper research and consultation, it's entirely manageable. By ensuring you meet these legal requirements, you'll be one step closer to running a successful, legally compliant café business. Always remember to check local regulations and consult with government agencies or legal professionals for guidance.

# CHAPTER 11:

Elevating Your Café Business: Innovative Approaches to Draw in Patrons

Achieving success in the café business necessitates more than merely offering excellent food and coffee. It demands thoughtful and dynamic promotional efforts to captivate customers and set your café apart from the competition. In this chapter, we will delve into diverse promotional strategies to bolster your café's visibility, clientele, and revenue.

Unearth Your Distinctive Value Proposition (DVP): Kick-off your promotional endeavors by discovering and emphasizing your distinctive value proposition. What makes your café uniquely attractive compared to others in the vicinity? Is it your artisan coffee, fresh pastries, welcoming ambiance, or superior customer service? Recognizing your DVP aids you in crafting appealing marketing narratives and luring customers who connect with your distinctive offerings.

Fortify Your Digital Footprint: An impressive online presence is crucial in today's digital age. Design a polished website to display your menu, ambiance, and contact details. Improve your website's search engine optimization to heighten its visibility in local search results. Also, harness the power of social media platforms such as Instagram, Facebook, and Twitter to engage with your target demographic. Share enticing photos of your café's offerings, update followers about events or specials, and promptly respond to customer feedback. Advocate for your patrons to share their café experiences on social media, thus amplifying your organic reach.

Optimize Local SEO Techniques: Use local SEO strategies to ensure your café tops local search results. Consistently update your business information across all platforms and motivate happy customers to leave positive reviews on platforms like Google My Business, Yelp, and TripAdvisor. Reviews play a significant role in swaying potential customers' choices.

Curate Engaging Events and Partnerships: Build excitement and draw in fresh faces by organizing engaging events or collaborations. Contemplate hosting live music evenings, art shows, book clubs, or partnering with local artists, musicians, or influencers. These activities not only attract new customers but also enrich your café's overall ambiance and reputation.

Institute Loyalty Programs and Exclusive Offers: Foster a loyal customer base by implementing reward programs. Offer incentives such as a free drink after a certain number of purchases or exclusive discounts for regular patrons. Create special deals or promotional periods during typically slower hours to boost sales, such as happy hour discounts, weekday lunch specials, or weekend brunch packages.

Form Partnerships with Local Businesses: Collaborate with local businesses that complement your café. You could offer a discount to customers who present a receipt from a nearby bookstore, gym, or boutique, and in turn, they could promote your café. These joint efforts help broaden your customer base and draw in new patrons who fit your target audience.

Integrate with the Community: Enhance your café's local reputation by becoming an active participant in community events, sponsoring local sports teams, or supporting charitable initiatives. This community integration fosters a sense of camaraderie and strengthens your brand's standing, making your café the go-to spot for locals.

Craft a Welcoming Environment: The ambiance of your café has a considerable impact on customer perception and their willingness to recommend your café. Ensure your space is clean, well-lit, and inviting with comfortable seating, soothing music, and decor that matches your brand's identity.

In conclusion, boosting your café business requires a combination of both digital and physical promotional strategies. By pinpointing your distinctive value proposition, crafting a strong digital footprint, engaging with the local community, and curating exclusive deals and events, you can cultivate a loyal customer base and set your café apart from the competition. Consistently apply these strategies, adapt based on customer feedback, and stay alert to evolving trends to ensure ongoing success in the dynamic café industry.

# CHAPTER 12:

A Symphony of Efficiency: Orchestrating a Smooth Café Experience

Navigating the bustling world of café management can feel like conducting an intricate symphony – there are countless notes to hit, harmonies to create, and the anticipation of an enraptured audience, your customers. To orchestrate a perfect performance, it's crucial to refine and tune your operations for peak efficiency. This chapter will delve into the art and science of fine-tuning café operations, transforming the act of serving coffee into a seamless, memorable ballet of taste and service.

A Focus on Efficiency: Transforming the Café Environment

In the quest for the quintessential café, efficiency is your guiding light. But it's more than just ticking tasks off a list. It breathes life into your café, cultivating an environment brimming with satisfaction, joy, and a sense of connection. How does efficiency contribute to a thriving café culture?

An Enthralling Customer Encounter: A well-oiled machine guarantees swift, accurate service, consistent quality and fosters customer loyalty.

Optimizing Resources: Efficiency helps eradicate wasteful practices, putting resources to their best use, and curtailing needless expenses.

Uplifting Team Spirit: A smooth-running café inspires its team, bolsters morale and job satisfaction.

Productivity Boom: By eradicating operational hindrances, productivity skyrockets, centering the focus on creating unforgettable customer experiences.

Decoding Current Café Practices: Identifying and Addressing Weak Spots

Before we jump headfirst into refining your café operations, it's vital to understand the current workings and discover potential room for improvement.

Spotting the Sore Points: Keep a watchful eye on the everyday running of your café, highlighting slow areas, communication hurdles, or inventory mishaps. Tackling these issues head-on is the first step to a smoother operation.

Employee Insights: Your team, being at the heart of your café operations, can provide valuable feedback. Establish a culture of open dialogue to gather their thoughts and suggestions.

Choreographing the Workflow: Standardizing and Systematizing

Achieving operational efficiency requires streamlining workflow processes.

Creating a Roadmap: Draft comprehensive standard operating procedures (SOPs) for every aspect of your café's workings. Training your staff to follow these SOPs ensures uniformity and smooth functioning.

Efficiency Tools: Embrace technology and tools designed to streamline operations, like a robust point-of-sale (POS) system, combining order taking, inventory, and report generation.

Building an Adept Team: Staffing and Training for Excellence

Assembling and training a proficient team is crucial to the flawless operation of your café.

Perfect Team Size: Evaluate your staffing needs by customer demand, peak hours, and seasonal trends. Avoid having too many or too few hands on deck, as it can affect efficiency and satisfaction levels.

Thorough Training: Create comprehensive training programs to equip your staff with required skills and knowledge, making them confident and adept at their roles.

Embracing the Future: Technology and Automation

Harness the power of modern technology to revolutionize your café operations.

POS Systems: Implement a modern POS system that automates order processing, tracks inventory, and gives insightful reports. This will streamline transactions and eradicate errors.

Online Convenience: Incorporate online ordering and reservations to manage customer flow, reduce wait times, and elevate the customer experience.

Harmonizing Communication and Collaboration

Establishing clear channels of communication and fostering collaboration can greatly enhance efficiency.

Open Dialogue: Encourage open communication among your team, be it through digital tools or team meetings, to promptly address issues and keep everyone updated.

Cross-Functional Team: Promote cross-training to develop a versatile team, enhancing operational flexibility and ensuring continuity during staff absences or peak times.

A Stellar Customer Experience: Efficiency with a Personal Touch

Efficiency should work hand in hand with exceptional customer service.

Speed and Accuracy: Efficient operations mean quicker service and accurate orders, giving customers a superior café experience.

Personal Touch: Train your staff to interact with customers on a more personal level, remembering their preferences, names, and special requests.

Checking the Pulse: Regular Performance Reviews

Consistent monitoring and evaluation of your café's performance ensure you stay on track.

Key Performance Indicators (KPIs): Establish KPIs, such as order processing time or customer satisfaction scores, and track them regularly to identify areas for improvement.

Feedback Sessions: Conduct regular reviews with your team to discuss performance, address concerns, and provide feedback. This promotes a culture of continuous learning and excellence.

Transforming your café operations into a finely-tuned symphony of efficiency is a dedicated and continuous process. It involves constant evaluation, strategic implementation, technology adoption, effective communication, and a deep-seated focus on the customer experience. By embracing this approach, you can conduct your café business to hit all the high notes, achieving success on an unprecedented scale.

# CHAPTER 13:

## Mastering the Intricacies of Inventory and Supplier Relations

Operating a cafe is an intricate dance of crafting tantalizing dishes, maintaining precise inventory levels, and nurturing robust relationships with trustworthy suppliers. The future of your cafe rests on the perfect alignment of these factors. In this chapter, we delve into the fundamental strategies for mastering inventory and supplier management, ultimately leading to a flawless operational flow and the delivery of top-tier quality to your patrons.

To flourish as a cafe entrepreneur, inventory and supplier management are pivotal to ensuring a frictionless experience for your customers. With the right stock quantities, high-grade ingredients, and a robust supplier network, you can enhance your cafe's workflow and amplify the satisfaction of your clientele.

Significance of Proficient Inventory and Supplier Management

Mastering inventory and supplier management is integral to your cafe's prosperity. Here's why:

Preventing shortages: Effective inventory management ensures you always have the required ingredients and supplies to cater to customer demand, thereby avoiding any possibility of running out.

Minimizing wastage: Optimum inventory control aids in reducing waste by thwarting overstocking or the spoilage of short-life items.

Guaranteeing consistency: Procuring ingredients from dependable suppliers ensures a uniform quality that enriches the dining experience for your customers.

Regulating costs: Efficacious inventory management minimizes costs by preventing excessive stock, refining purchasing decisions, and negotiating superior pricing with suppliers.

Scrutinizing Inventory Requirements

Before plunging into inventory management, take time to gauge your unique inventory needs based on your menu offerings and customer demand. Consider the following:

Identifying Key Menu Items: Recognize the staple dishes on your menu and the ingredients needed for their preparation. Categorize items according to popularity and consumption frequency to prioritize your inventory necessities.

Projecting Demand: Leverage historical data, sales patterns, and customer feedback to estimate the demand for different menu items. This information will guide your purchasing decisions, preventing stock shortages or surplus.

Establishing Trustworthy Supplier Connections

Identifying and forming alliances with trustworthy suppliers is vital to uphold the quality and consistency of your cafe's offerings. Take into account the following steps:

Surveying Suppliers: Carry out comprehensive research to pinpoint potential suppliers in your vicinity. Look for those specializing in the products you need, with a proven track record of reliability and quality. Request samples, compare prices, and gather recommendations from other businesses before finalizing your decision.

Cultivating Relationships: Foster relationships with your suppliers through transparent communication and trust-building. Communicate your needs regularly, provide feedback on product quality, and promptly address any concerns. Strong supplier relationships can yield improved service, priority access to products, and potential cost benefits.

Inventory Oversight and Surveillance

Maintaining control over your inventory is a cornerstone of efficient operations. Ponder over the following practices:

Establishing Minimum Stock Levels: Set minimum stock levels (par levels) for each inventory item to ward off stock shortages. Keep a close eye on inventory levels and reorder items when they fall to the designated par levels.

Routine Stock Checks and Reorders: Execute regular stock checks to ensure inventory accuracy and uncover any discrepancies. Implement a systematic reorder procedure, ensuring you have sufficient lead time to receive new shipments before depleting crucial items.

Maintaining Quality and Shelf Life

To serve exceptional quality to your customers, pay attention to the shelf life and product freshness:

Utilizing FIFO Method: Adhere to the FIFO (First-In, First-Out) method, which implies using the oldest inventory items first to guarantee freshness and reduce wastage. Properly rotate inventory to avoid spoilage or expiration of ingredients.

Observing Proper Storage Rules: Follow correct storage procedures for different ingredients, including temperature control and separation of perishable and non-perishable items. Train your staff on the right handling and rotation techniques to preserve quality and prevent product loss.

Ordering and Delivery Process Optimization

Revamp your ordering and delivery processes for time-saving and error reduction:

Order Placement Efficiency: Leverage technology or online platforms for efficient order placement with your suppliers. Implement standardized order forms or templates to ensure precision and provide clear instructions to your suppliers.

Delivery Monitoring: Regularly check delivery timings and inspect the quality of items upon arrival. Promptly address any issues and maintain open communication with your suppliers to rectify problems or tweak future orders as necessary.

Mitigating Supply Chain Risks

Recognize potential risks in your supply chain and develop contingency plans:

Risk Identification: Assess potential risks such as supplier disruptions, price fluctuations, natural disasters, or regulatory changes. Stay abreast of industry trends and maintain alternate suppliers or sourcing options to mitigate potential risks.

Contingency Planning: Develop contingency plans for potential disruptions in your supply chain. These plans might include alternative suppliers, backup inventory storage, or temporary menu adjustments in case of ingredient unavailability.

Harnessing Technology and Automation

Utilize technology to simplify inventory and supplier management:

Inventory Management Systems: Consider using an inventory management system to automate inventory tracking, restocking, and forecasting. These systems provide real-time data, generate reports, and optimize inventory levels based on historical and current demand.

Digital Ordering and Invoicing: Use digital systems for order placement and invoicing to cut down on paperwork, streamline processes, and reduce errors. Digital systems also provide accurate records for expense tracking and accounting simplification.

Proficient inventory and supplier management are fundamental for your cafe's smooth operation and success. By assessing your inventory needs, sourcing reliable suppliers, implementing effective processes, and harnessing technology, you can assure consistent quality, reduce waste, and optimize costs. Remember, managing your inventory and suppliers is a continuous process that demands vigilance and constant enhancement.

# CHAPTER 14:

## The Art of Orchestrating Your Cafe Finances

Owning a cafe is much more than being the creator of enchanting flavors; it's also about the meticulous orchestration of your financial resources. An absence of proficient financial planning can render your cafe vulnerable to fiscal issues, hinder its expansion, and obstruct profitability. In this chapter, we'll take a deep dive into the heart of financial planning and management for a prosperous cafe business.

Embarking on the journey of owning a cafe is a dream come true for many, but it is crucial to step onto this path with a well-structured financial strategy. By comprehending and managing your finances efficiently, you are setting a robust foundation for your cafe's lasting success and stability.

Building a Financial Blueprint A carefully crafted financial blueprint serves as the bedrock of any thriving cafe business. Here are some strategic steps to contemplate:

Gauging Initial Expenditure Kick-start by pinpointing and evaluating the sundry costs involved in launching your cafe. These expenditures include lease or acquisition of a location, equipment, decor, permits and licenses, beginning inventory, and promotional activities. An accurate approximation of your initial costs will help you determine the extent of capital you need to amass.

Forecasting Recurring Costs Once your cafe takes off, it will be accompanied by recurring expenses that require your attention. These involve mortgage or rent payments, utility bills, payroll, inventory replenishment, advertising, maintenance, and other running costs. Anticipating and allocating a budget for these costs will aid in sustaining your cafe's fiscal health.

Establishing Revenue Objectives For a pragmatic financial blueprint, you must establish revenue objectives rooted in market research, competition analysis, and your target audience. Gauge factors like average customer expenditure, sales volume, and pricing strategy. Setting realistic revenue objectives enables you to track your progress and make necessary tweaks.

Garnering Capital Capital is a critical pillar of establishing and nurturing a cafe business. Here are some avenues to consider:

Self-Investment Contemplate infusing your personal savings or assets into the cafe. This demonstrates your devotion and commitment to the venture. However, carefully analyze your financial state and associated risks before committing personal funds.

Debt Financing Examine different debt financing options accessible for small enterprises, such as business loans, credit lines, or equipment financing. Scrutinize the terms, interest rates, and repayment schedules to identify the financing solution best suited for your cafe.

Venture Capital If additional capital is required, you can seek venture capitalists interested in your cafe venture. Develop an engaging business plan and presentation to attract potential investors that align with your vision. Bear in mind that venture capital involves sharing ownership and profits.

Budgeting and Cost Management Apt budgeting and cost management are imperative for fiscal stability and growth. Contemplate the following:

Expense Monitoring Maintain an exhaustive record of all your cafe-related expenditures. This includes fixed (e.g., rent, utilities) and variable costs (e.g., inventory, promotions). Periodically review your expenditures to spot potential areas for cost optimization.

Cost Management Deploy strategies to manage costs without sacrificing quality. This could involve striking favorable deals with suppliers, optimizing staffing to limit overtime, and introducing energy-efficient practices to curb utility costs.

Strategic Fund Allocation Strategically distribute your funds to areas that substantially impact your cafe's success. This could involve investing in premium ingredients, staff development, marketing initiatives, or upgrading equipment. Prioritize expenditures based on their potential return on investment.

Financial Projections and Forecasting To remain financially on track, devise precise financial projections and forecasts:

Revenue Forecasting Project your future revenue by analyzing historical data, market trends, and customer behavior. Consider factors like seasonality, local events, and external factors influencing customer visits. Regularly revise your revenue forecasts to accommodate changing scenarios.

Cash Flow Estimation Maintain a cash flow estimate to predict the timing of cash inflows and outflows. This helps you ensure enough liquidity to cover expenses, invest when necessary, and handle revenue variations.

Adjusting for Seasonality If your cafe sees seasonal variations in sales, adjust your financial projections accordingly. Plan for lean periods by reserving funds during high seasons to cover costs during slower times.

Risk Mitigation and Contingency Planning Financial risk management is crucial for your cafe's long-term success:

Insurance Ensure your cafe and its assets are protected with appropriate insurance coverage.

This may encompass general liability insurance, property insurance, workers' compensation, and business interruption insurance. Consult with an insurance professional to ensure comprehensive coverage for potential risks.

Emergency Fund Reserve emergency funds to deal with unexpected costs or temporary financial setbacks. A safety net can provide peace of mind and help you navigate through obstacles without compromising daily operations.

Risk Mitigation Identify potential financial risks, such as changes in market demand, supply chain disruptions, or regulatory modifications. Develop contingency strategies to address these risks and minimize their impact on your cafe's fiscal stability.

Professional Assistance Don't hesitate to seek professional help for managing your cafe's finances:

Financial Experts Consider employing a skilled accountant or bookkeeper to manage your financial documentation, tax obligations, and financial reporting. They can offer valuable insights and ensure adherence to financial regulations.

Financial Consultants Engage a financial consultant to assist you with informed decisions about investments, loans, and long-term financial strategies. Their expertise can help you maximize profits and navigate financial challenges.

Legal Support Consult a legal expert specializing in small business law to ensure compliance with relevant regulations and contracts. They can help navigate legal intricacies and safeguard your cafe's financial interests.

The success of your cafe is heavily reliant on effective planning and management of its finances. By developing a comprehensive financial plan, securing funding, budgeting efficiently, and seeking professional help, you can confidently steer through the financial aspects of running your cafe. Remember, rigorous financial management is the key to profitability and fostering growth.

# EPILOGUE:

Well done! You've journeyed to the closing pages of this comprehensive guide on establishing a cafe, and are now armed with the wisdom and resources needed to embark on this exhilarating voyage into the world of entrepreneurship. Initiating a cafe isn't a walk in the park, but with meticulous strategizing, unwavering commitment, and a fervor for curating unforgettable moments, your vision can transition into a prosperous venture.

In the course of this guide, we've traversed an array of subjects, from architecting a robust business blueprint to discerning your ideal clientele, from concocting a palate-pleasing menu to deploying impactful promotional tactics. We've dug deep into the operational nitty-gritty of managing a cafe, encompassing team building, fiscal mapping, and risk evaluation.

Starting a cafe is more than offering exceptional food and beverages; it's about cultivating a warm environment, nurturing a communal spirit, and delivering an extraordinary level of customer care. Your cafe should evolve into a sanctuary where patrons feel at ease, a space where they can relax, engage with peers, and partake in gastronomic pleasures.

As you set sail on this journey, bear in mind that the path might be strewn with hurdles. Building a devoted customer following might demand time, and roadblocks may appear. But with tenacity, versatility, and an openness to perpetual learning and enhancement, you can surmount these impediments and realize enduring success.

Don't shy away from pioneering ideas, daring innovations, and actualizing your distinct dream. Value your customers' input and tweak your services to mirror their preferences. Keep abreast of the industry's latest trends, and consistently strive for perfection in every facet of your cafe.

Recognize that you are part of a supportive network. Draw upon the wisdom of mentors, industry guilds, and peer cafe proprietors who can offer direction and share their anecdotes. Partner with local vendors, craftsmen, and community initiatives to nurture robust alliances and contribute to the development of your community.

Launching a cafe is a testament to your love and dedication. It demands grit, toil, and an authentic zeal for your craft. But the rewards are beyond quantification. The elation of witnessing your customers' pleasure as they relish your gourmet offerings, the gratification of steering a flourishing enterprise, and the ties you weave with your community - all these enrich your journey immeasurably.

Hence, step forward with assurance, fortified with the insight and motivation gleaned from this guide. Believe in your capacity. Embrace the obstacles, savor the victories, and remember that establishing a cafe isn't merely about serving food and drinks - it's about crafting a haven where folks can congregate, bond, and create cherished memories.

Best wishes on your expedition to create a buzzing and adored cafe. May your enthusiasm and diligence yield success and gratification beyond your wildest imagination. Toast to your forthcoming venture!